Strength in Numbers

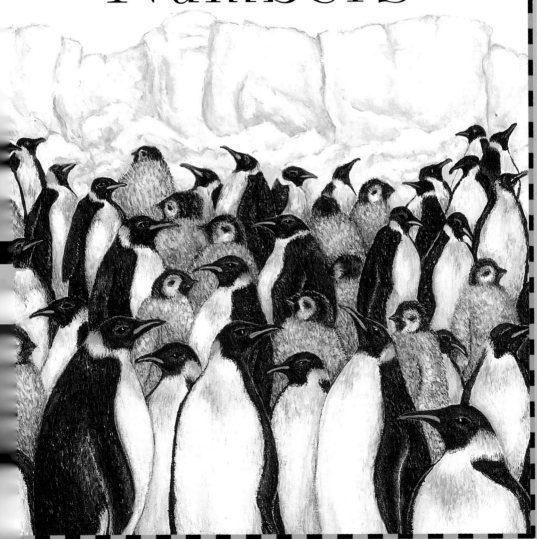

Contents

Features

If you think *ladybird* is a strange name, turn to page 6 to see what this little beetle is called in other countries.

Read about the damage caused by swarms of locusts. Then find out what locals mean when they say, "If you can't beat them, eat them!" in **Swarm Warning** on page 10.

For the inside story on an insect that uses teamwork to build a nest taller than an elephant, see **Master Builders** on page 18.

How many eggs does a spider lay? Turn to page 21 for fascinating facts.

How is an insect colony like a city?
Visit www.infosteps.co.uk
for more about BEES AND WASPS.

Safety in Numbers

Many animals live in large groups. Living in a group makes it easier to defend the herd or pack. Because a **predator** has many animals from which to choose, most group members have time to escape. Living in a group also means it is easier to find a mate and there are more helpers to care for the young.

Wildebeest have good hearing but poor smell. Zebras have a good sense of smell. Together they can warn each other of predators.

Meerkats live together in packs. When a meerkat spots a predator it lets out a shrill cry. The pack then escapes to the safety of its underground burrows.

5

Shelter in Numbers

Penguins and gulls often nest in colonies of thousands of birds. Living in a colony, where many animals are watching for predators, keeps the chicks safe.

Ladybirds do not usually live in a group. However, they gather into a **swarm** to make their own shelter at the end of summer. They **hibernate** together through the cold weather.

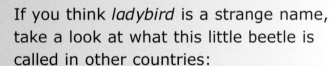

WORD BUILDER

If you think *ladybird* is a strange name, take a look at what this little beetle is called in other countries:
- Flower Lady (China)
- Water Delivery-Man's Daughter (Iraq)
- Indra's Cowherd (India)
- Crop Picker (Africa)
- Good News (Iran)

Zebra stripes make it difficult for a predator to see one zebra in a herd. They also make it hard to see the outline of just one zebra. The stripes seem to make the zebra "fade" at its edges.

Power in Numbers

Many insects find strength in numbers. Some insects are powerful or even dangerous only because they work in groups. The sting of one killer bee is no worse than the sting of any other kind of bee. However, killer bees defend themselves by attacking in huge numbers. Killer bees are very dangerous because they work in large groups.

One African driver ant is harmless. However, these ants can travel in swarms of 20 million! When a large swarm attacks it kills everything in its path.

Swarm Warning

Locusts usually live alone. However, they gather in groups and **migrate** to new feeding grounds when there is not enough food. A swarm of locusts can contain a million insects per hectare. With "strength in numbers", swarms can fly 5,000 kilometres in five days, eating everything they can find.

Sometimes swarms of locusts are so big they shut out the sunlight. They can also make travelling in aeroplanes, cars and trains dangerous.

A locust swarm means disaster for this farmer in West Africa.

If You Can't Beat Them, Eat Them!

Some people have decided that if locusts eat their crops they will eat the locusts!

A Locust Recipe Used in Cambodia

Step 1 Take 30 to 40 dead adult locusts.

Step 2 Slit the abdomen lengthwise. Stuff a peanut inside.

Step 3 Lightly fry the locusts in a wok or frying pan. Add oil and salt to taste. Be careful not to burn the locusts.

Step 4 Enjoy!

Hunting in Numbers

Many animals such as lions, hyenas, wolves and wild dogs work together to find food. By hunting in groups of up to twenty members they are able to catch and kill larger **prey**. Some animals such as African hunting dogs also hunt and eat in packs so every animal in the group gets enough food.

In a pride of lions the lionesses do the hunting. Then they share their prey with the rest of the pride.

Team Power

Some ocean animals such as orca also hunt together. One orca may frighten a group of seals by coming very close to shore. The seals then try to escape into the sea where other orca are waiting.

Humpback whales work together to herd schools of fish. The group of whales split up and surround the fish. The fish are then trapped.

Sea lions
often hunt squid
or fish together.
When predators work
as a group they have
a better chance
of catching prey.

Working as a Team

Bees, wasps, ants and termites may be small, but they make up for their size by living together in colonies. Every member of a colony has an important job to do. The queen spends her whole life laying eggs. Workers look after the eggs, find food and raise the young. In ant and termite colonies soldiers defend the nest. All workers and soldiers are female. The males' job is to start new colonies with young queens.

Male bees are called drones

SITESEEING
PLANTS & ANIMALS

How is an insect colony like a city?

Visit **www.infosteps.co.uk**
for more about BEES AND WASPS.

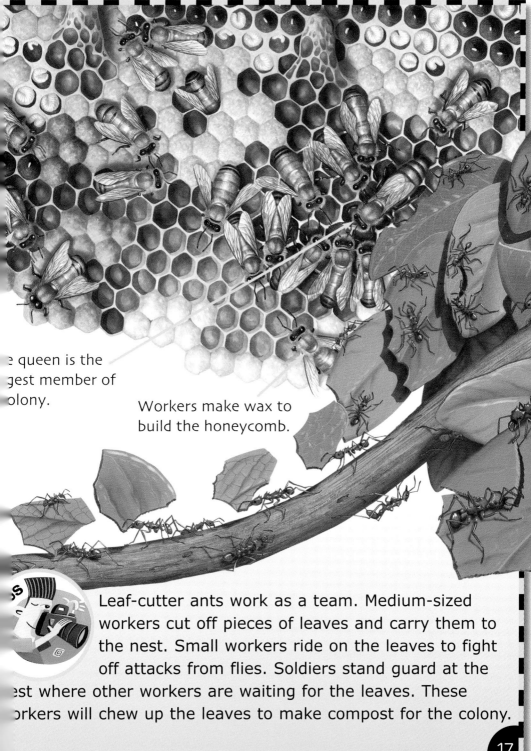

queen is the
gest member of
olony.

Workers make wax to
build the honeycomb.

Leaf-cutter ants work as a team. Medium-sized
workers cut off pieces of leaves and carry them to
the nest. Small workers ride on the leaves to fight
off attacks from flies. Soldiers stand guard at the
est where other workers are waiting for the leaves. These
orkers will chew up the leaves to make compost for the colony.

Master Builders

Of all animals termites are the master builders. Termites work together to build huge, strong nests called mounds. Termite mounds can be 6 metres tall and go deep underground. Scientists think that some mounds may have been used for more than 4,000 years.

Termite mounds are carefully planned. They have many tunnels to keep fresh air flowing. This is similar to built-in air conditioning.

Around the world termites build different kinds of nes. This termite mound is in Western Australia.

Inside a Termite Mound

The queen termite is much bigger than the other termites. In her lifetime she may lay 14 million eggs.

Termites grow their own fungus gardens for food.

t air escapes m the nest ough tunnels. ol air is sucked rom the und below.

rkers look r the s and ng in series.

ier nites ect nest.

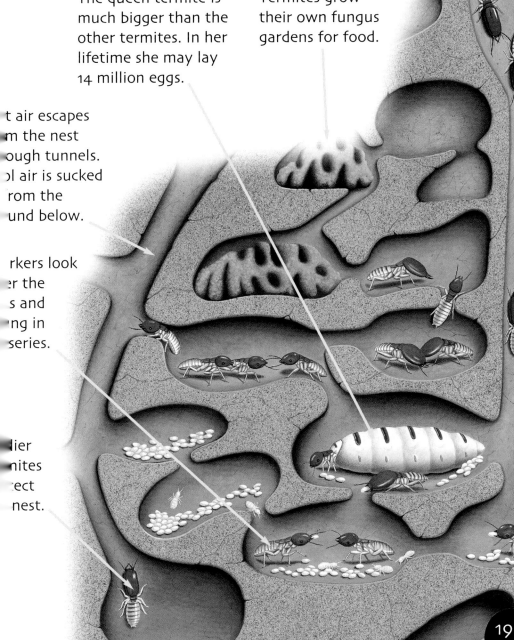

Numbers for Survival

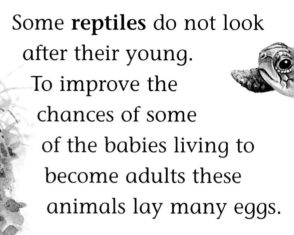

Some **reptiles** do not look after their young. To improve the chances of some of the babies living to become adults these animals lay many eggs.

Female sea turtles lay up to 200 eggs at a time. Both the eggs and hatchlings are the prey of many animals. On the way to the sea many your turtles are eaten by birds and crabs. Those hatchlings that reach the sea may then be the prey of sharks and other fish.

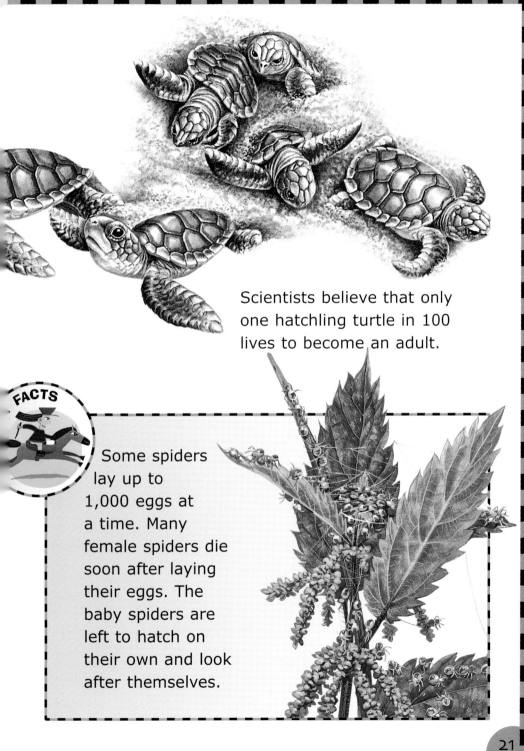

Scientists believe that only one hatchling turtle in 100 lives to become an adult.

FACTS

Some spiders lay up to 1,000 eggs at a time. Many female spiders die soon after laying their eggs. The baby spiders are left to hatch on their own and look after themselves.

Glossary

hibernate – to rest in a state similar to a very deep sleep. Many animals hibernate through the winter when food is hard to find.

migrate – to move from one country or area to another. Locusts migrate when they don't have enough food. Many birds migrate to warmer areas for the winter.

predator – an animal that lives by killing and eating other animals

prey – an animal that is hunted and eaten by another animal

reptile – a cold-blooded animal that crawls on its belly or creeps on short legs. Many reptiles lay eggs and do not look after their young.

swarm – a large number of insects moving as a group

Index

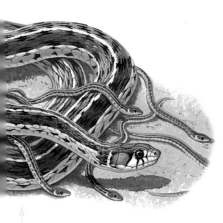

Discussion Starters

1 Sometimes people also rely on strength in numbers. What are two ways people use the strength, safety or cooperation of a large group?

2 Some animals do not use strength in numbers. What are two kinds of animals that live by themselves or in small family groups? Why don't they need the safety of a large group?

3 Out of all the animals discussed in this book which do you admire the most? Why?